Dunfermline and Rosyth
in old picture postcards volume 2

by Eric Simpson and George Robertson

European Library ZALTBOMMEL/THE NETHERLANDS

The authors

Eric Simpson was born in Buckie and is a graduate of Aberdeen University. A former Head of History at Moray House College in Edinburgh, he has lived at Dalgety Bay in Fife since 1966. His other books include 'Discovering Banff, Moray & Nairn' (John Donald), 'The Vikings in Scotland', 'Dalgety – the story of a parish', and 'The Auld Grey Toun – Dunfermline in the time of Andrew Carnegie 1835-1919'. He is the author, too, of the following European Library publications – namely, 'Aberdour and Burntisland in old picture postcards', 'Inverkeithing and Dalgety in old picture postcards' (with George Hastie).

Eric Simpson and George Robertson have collaborated on three previous European Library works – 'Dunfermline and Rosyth in old picture postcards', 'Cowdenbeath in old picture postcards' and 'Limekilns to Culross in old picture postcards'.

George Robertson, Rosyth born and bred, has lived in the Dunfermline area all his life. He is a former Police Inspector with Fife Constabulary. During his police service, he was stationed, in the main, at Dunfermline and Rosyth. Currently employed at the Andrew Carnegie Birthplace and Museum in Dunfermline, he is chairman of Dunfermline Historical Society and is also a voluntary guide for Dunfermline Heritage Trust.

Acknowledgements

We are grateful to those people who loaned us material and/or assisted in other ways. While it would be impossible to list every person who helped in one way or another, special thanks must be paid to the following: Alan Brotchie, Edith May, Nadia Maloco, Andrew Mitchell, George Luke, Domenica Cascarino, Andrew Mackie, Charles Finlay, John Kennedy, Mrs. G.L. Beveridge, David Harrison, Dorothy Hall, Willi Henderson, Jim Craig, Jimmy Dick, Martin Rogers, Betty Lawrence, Cathy Taylor, Douglas Scott, Cathy Paton, George Hastie and Fraser Simpson. Chris Neale, Penny Maplesden and other Dunfermline Library staff have provided valuable help and assistance. We are also greatly indebted to our wives Kathleen and Maureen for proofreading and encouragement. For permission to reproduce photographs, we must also thank the Royal Commission on the Ancient and Historical Monuments of Scotland for Nos. 102 and 113 and D.L.G. Hunter for Nos. 58 and 122.

GB ISBN 90 288 6316 8

© 1996 European Library – Zaltbommel/The Netherlands

Eric Simpson / George Robertson

Introduction

Over the years quite a number of photographers have recorded the passing scene. While some have been amateurs, others have worked on a professional basis. The results of their endeavours, whether amateur snapshots or highly professional images, have provided us with the raw material for this illustrated depiction of times of change in the Auld Grey Toun of Dunfermline. The proprietor of the first 'photographic establishment' in Dunfermline was a Mr. Louis. Although we cannot point to any specific examples of his work, we can be sure that portraits, or likenesses, would have been his staple. How much business he did in 1854 when he started up is open to question. It was a time of trade depression and 500 men were out of work. Yet change was afoot. The town of Dunfermline (population some 13,000) was now connected to the railway system. In industry, too, the power of steam was being demonstrated to full effect. The first successful power loom machines were then at work in factories in Pilmuir Street and in St. Leonard's. The day of the traditional hand-loom weaver was coming to an end.

Other photographers came and went. Some prospered and survived much longer than the average. James Norval was one who made his mark not just as a very professional photographer and businessman, but also, as a number of the photographs and captions in this volume confirm, as one of the burgh's leading citizens. It was in 1885 that James Norval set up business in his own right, having previously managed a studio for a Kirkcaldy-based firm. Prospects must have seemed good. The burgh population was rising, now up to around the 15,000 mark. Dunfermline had now a direct rail link to Edinburgh via a railway ferry from North Queensferry to Port Edgar. Work, too, had started on a massive new project – a great new rail bridge to span the Forth at Queensferry. New linen mills had been built to meet the demand, at both home and abroad, for high-quality damask table-linen and other like products.

New types of camera and new photographic processes increased the number, though not always the quality, of photographic images. In 1911 an American Midget Photo Company was advertising its services in Chalmers Street, Dunfermline. By then the transport network had seen further change with the opening in 1909 of the electric tramway system. Even more significant was the decision by the British Admiralty to build a naval base at Rosyth. Work on this base and its associated dockyard, though, did not get underway until 1909. The outbreak of war in 1914 ensured that the work of construction was considerably accelerated. The planners, too, saw the need for a large number of dwellings to house the employees of the dockyard. In 1910, therefore, a decision was made to build a new settlement on the then fashionable 'garden city' principles. The new suburb, the so-called Rosyth Garden City, was brought within the now extended boundaries of the ancient royal burgh of Dunfermline. Local photographers gained business, too, from tourists and other visitors to the Auld Grey Toun. Tourists were drawn to the burgh for its wealth of history, for the Andrew Carnegie connection, and for the town's prime new visitor attraction, Pittencrieff Park, which was one of Carnegie's most notable philanthropic gifts to the town of his birth. As many of the illustrations both in this book and in the preceding volume clearly show, Pittencrieff Glen proved to be a photographer's mecca.

The photographic record reflects social change and reveals the extent of the physical transformation of the town. Some of these changes arose not because of local choice, but sprang instead from events and circumstances far removed from the Auld Grey Toun. It was the rise of Germany as a naval power which brought Rosyth into being. At the end of the Great War, the balance of power had changed once again. The German High Seas Fleet was scuttled at Scapa Flow and no longer posed a threat. In 1925, therefore, the British naval establishment abandoned Rosyth and retreated to its traditional south of England bases. With Rosyth reduced to a 'care and maintenance' basis, part of this expensively-equipped dockyard was transformed, as photograph No. 102 shows, into a demolition yard. The renewal of the German naval threat meant that Rosyth was reactivated immediately prior to the outbreak of the Second World War in 1939. The aerial menace meant that the nearby Donibristle air base was likewise reactivated (see Nos. 94 and 95).

It was in 1939 too, the year the war started, that Herbert T. Macpherson moved his business to the Regal Close. The photograph taken of his new shop shows that picture postcards were still a good line of business. (See No. 12.) Local shopkeepers, like Macpherson, were eager to have their names embossed on a variety of cards. Once the war had started, shortages of materials and the need for military secrecy meant that much wartime activity went unrecorded. As in the First World War (see the section on Rosyth), photographs were taken for propaganda reasons and for other official purposes. We find, in addition, photographs of men and women in uniform being taken for commemorative purposes, as for example Nos. 83b and 120.

When peace came in 1945, there were fears that, as in 1925, the Rosyth base and dockyard would once again be declared surplus to requirements. The onset of the Cold War ensured that Rosyth was retained to help counter the naval threat from the Soviet Union. When the Cold War was over, Rosyth once more was threatened with extinction. Today, the privatised dockyard of Rosyth employs a much reduced workforce. Compared with former days (see No. 32), the naval presence is now derisory. The last vessels to be based at Rosyth, some minor war vessels, left for other ports in November 1995.

When in 1854 Mr. Louis established his photographic studio, the camera was an exciting innovation, but one which was the preserve of a few professionals and a handful of dedicated, and wealthy, amateurs. In recent years, with personal cameras now commonplace, very many more people are providing material for the photographic record. For the last decades of the 20th century, we have a huge choice of visual material – ranging from snapshots of family and friends to portraits and other photographs taken by highly skilled professionals. They do, though, tell a story and all are part of the photographic record of Dunfermline and surrounding area. From Victorian days to more recent times, we thus possess a permanent visual record of days that have departed and of places that have gone or have been changed out of all recognition.

1   We start at the top of the New Row around 1920. DCI stands for Dick's Co-operative Institutions (see pictures 7 and 121 in volume I). Judging by the amount of meat on display, there was evidently no BSE scare at that time. There is a DCI baker's shop next door and above a dental establishment. This was obviously a photo taken for advertising purposes, since posed outside are some counter staff and delivery men with their vans. The solid-tyred motor vehicle is open at the front, just like the horse-drawn van. The corner shop was taken over in 1954 by Grafton's, ladies' outfitters.

2   Here we see a tram of the Dunfermline and District Tramways Company. The time is the early 1920s, the location is the East Port loop (a passing place) and the tram has come from Lochore. The tramway system was extended to Lochore in 1912. On the left, we see the former St. Margaret's Parish Church, which was demolished to make way for a new office building for Dunfermline Building Society. Apart from the shop signs, the buildings, as far as we can see, are little changed.

3   We come to another loop section on the tramway line leading into Dunfermline from Halbeath. The year is 1925 and the motor-car and lamp-posts are very much of that period. Although the sun is shining and the street seems dry, the youngster on the right is kitted out ready for monsoon conditions. The shop on the extreme left, with a lassie keeking roon the corner, advertises the services of William Laing & Son, Dyers & Cleaners, Alloa. The dwellings in the far distance are now gone. The cupola-topped building on the other corner was erected in 1904 by the Dunfermline Co-operative Society. The message states that he (or maybe it is a she!) has been awarded the degree of F.E.I.S. (Fellow of the Educational Institute of Scotland). The sender wanted the Edinburgh recipient to reserve a seat for a matinee performance of George Bernard Shaw's play 'St. Joan'.

Appin Crescent East, Dunfermline.

4 In this greatly-altered scene, we observe the Town-hill tram passing the Public Park gates. The prominent building to the left is the Park Tavern, which was demolished to make way for the much-maligned Sinclair Gardens roundabout. Recreational open spaces as 'lungs' for the working populace were very much in vogue in mid-Victorian Britain. We can trace the origin of the Dunfermline Public Park to a notice in a local newspaper dated June 1861, stating that 'a party' wished to purchase a piece of ground for the recreation of the inhabitants and the drilling of the local Volunteers. The Public Park, designed by Sir Joseph Paxton of Crystal Palace fame, was eventually opened to the public in 1863. The bandstand, a gift from Mrs. Louise Carnegie, was added in 1888.

The Park Gates, Dunfermline.

WITH LOTS · O' LUCK
The Tartan fair brings hame aince mair,
Sweet thochts o' the dear auld Hame,
For, though suns aye shine in a foreign clime,
Scotland's the dearest name

· CLAN · MACDONALD

5   Now Robins Cinema (left) this 1913 Art Deco edifice was the first purpose-built picture-house in Dunfermline. Eventually, other larger and more imposing cinemas were opened in the town, but The Cinema, as it was then, is the only one still showing films. Going from East Port to Reform Street, we arrive at the Opera House (right) which was designed as a two-balconied theatre. Opened in 1903, this lavish 1250 seat theatre was rather pretentiously described as the Theatre Royal Opera House. Early advertising stated that it was 'visited only by Companies of the Highest Repute... and was the Only Recognised Theatre in Fife'. Patrons were advised that a late train ran to Thornton and intermediate stations every Saturday at 10.39 p.m. Observe the street signs indicating that there was a pub, the Station Tavern, on the left and just beyond the Opera House, the old Queen Anne School entrance.

6   Greatly altered and now known as Carnegie Drive, Reform Street is no more. This name dates back to the 19th century, to the time of the great popular demonstrations for parliamentary reform. Notice how crowded the street scene is. The photograph must have been taken at the change-over. There is a queue at one side of the street, waiting for the next performance, and a stream of customers leaving the theatre. With competition from TV and other new forms of entertainment, the Opera House became redundant and was closed in 1955 and the building turned to other use. Despite public protest, the ornate interior was removed and transported for theatrical use to Sarasota in Florida. The Opera House was then demolished in 1982. Other weel-kent establishments include MacBay, fishmonger, and Dobie, saddler.

7   Still in Reform Street but now across the road from Dobie's, we come to the fish restaurant belonging to Mrs. Angelantonio Cascarino. The date is early September and the year is 1920, as confirmed by the poster in the window which tells us what was running at The Cinema. The films include 'The Career of Katherine Bush', 'Masked Rider', 'The Great Gamble', and 'Square Deal Sanderson' – this last a Western romance starring William S. Hart. Another notice laments that the proprietrix had been compelled to increase prices. Fish and chips then cost 7 d – at that price presumably seated in the restaurant! Mrs. A. Cascarino (Domenica) stands to the left. Notice the bashful bairn to the rear – identity unknown. Domenica came to Scotland in 1912 from Frosinone in Italy with her husband and eldest child Bascaleno (Bashie), then six years old.

8   This is an older photograph showing the Cascarino family not long after their arrival in Scotland. Cascarino senior is in the cart selling ginger beer. 'CAN'T BE BEAT' is the slogan on the roof of the vehicle. The location could be the Coal Road. Notice the candy twist roof support of another vehicle, just visible on the right. Domenica on the right is holding a container of some sorts while the young Bashie seems to be eating – chips?

9   Bashie Cascarino is now a young man working for himself with his name adorning his ice-cream cairt, as we see in the street view (above). Selling wafers and sponges, he boasts of his 'HIGH CLASS ICES'. The same horse (Peggy was her name) appears in the lower photo. This photograph was probably taken at a local fair. Note, adjacent to Bashie's cairt, a wooden caravan and a fenced-off tent with a notice which reads: 'The First Visit Of The Old Gypsy Queen.' As the placard indicates, she was a palmist. Bashie (1906-1990) was an amateur boxer, which explains why in later years he had a bit of a flattened nose. He was well-known for his generosity and open-handedness.

10   Back now to the New Row, we see another greatly changed street scene. We are looking up towards the High Street from the Central Auction Market (right). On the High Street/Bonnar Street corner, we note another shop – James Dick, grocer's, which was the forerunner of the DCI. It is reputed to be the first shop in the town to have electric light. Beyond on the Inglis Street corner, we see the Union Inn.

11 This early 20th century view of the High Street reveals that Craig's bakery shop on the extreme left sold Dunfermline Abbey Rock. (There was also a Carnegie Rock and Robert the Bruce Shortbread.) The next shop, Dan Thomson's, displays external clocks. He was of course a watchmaker and jeweller. This business survived until 1974. The adjacent two-storey building was demolished in 1931 to make way for the new Regal picture-house. The next block shows a sign advertising 'FINEST ICES & BILLIARDS'. These premises belonged to Angelo Maloco. (See volume I captions 28 and 29.) On the sunny side of the street, the sunshades are up and, a sign of changing times, two of the ladies have dispensed with hats.

High Street, Dunfermline.

12   Craig's bakehouse, which was located in the Regal Close, was taken over by Herbert T. Macpherson who was flitting premises from the nearby High Street. This photograph, taken seemingly just after the outbreak of war in September 1939, shows a very crowded window display and a number of external display boards and postcard racks. Indeed a number of the postcards reproduced in this book, and our previous one, were published by Herbert T. Macpherson under the trade name of the Herbert Series. Note the variety of goods and services provided. Books on sale included 'Gone with the Wind' (5/-), 'Just William', and Pear's Encyclopaedia (cost 2/6). An obviously new poster exhorts customers to withstand the rigours of the wartime blackout by purchasing Waddington's Indoor Games, including Monopoly, Totopoly, and Lexington. Beside the door there was a paper rack with only one magazine on it – the autumn number of Punch (price 1/). Even the rubber mat in the doorway carries an advertisement. Customers are invited to 'Ask for Stephen's Fountain Pen Ink'.

13   Back on the High Street, we are now at the foot of Douglas Street. One of the posters at the newsagent's door gives us the approximate date. It refers to a speech by Lord Kitchener regarding the duration of the war. Kitchener was Secretary for War from August 1914 until his death in June 1916. It is worth noting that the postcard publisher emphasised their patriotism by stating that their cards were guaranteed to be of British manufacture. Prior to the Great War, most postcards were printed in Germany. Are the gents scanning their newspapers (on the right) reading about the war or the racing results? The tramcar has come from Lochore and is heading west towards Rumblingwell.

High Street, Dunfermline

14 Proceeding west, we arrive at Hepworths, a chain gents' outfitters. Other firms, in this early 1930s card, include, on the left, the Bruce Restaurant and Café with baker's shop on the ground floor and, on the right, Greenlees & Sons, shoemakers. All these firms have now departed from Dunfermline, except for Boots, who then occupied a small store next to Bruce the baker's. The direction the cars are facing remind us that two-way traffic was then the norm. One-way traffic was introduced to Dunfermline in 1951.

HIGH STREET, DUNFERMLINE.

15   In this early 1950s post-card, we see yet more multiples – including Woolies, which crossed the road in 1938 (see volume I, pictures 1 to 3). Other multiples were the Fifty Shillings Tailor's and Claude Alexander's (yet another gents' tailor). These stores have gone, as has C. Smith & Sons, pork butcher's. By this time, too, the tramcars had gone.

HIGH STREET, DUNFERMLINE

16   Now we go back in time to 1911, when the Coronation proclamation of George V was made with great pomp and circumstance. The ceremony is taking place on the High Street outside the guildhall (now the Job Centre). Note the then location of the mercat cross and the oddly-placed ornamental gas street lamp. It is no wonder that the suffragette movement was so active at that time, for there is not one woman on the platform. But women and children were graciously permitted to spectate from the first floor windows. While the Provost, Robert Husband, wears his official garb, the other toon councillors and important guests wear the obligatory top hat and frock coat.

17   Looking towards the Toon Hoose, we see a box-shaped cart in the distance and on the left a milk lorry. The be-gaitered milkman is serving a laddie, tilting the milk churn towards him in the process. It was common practice for customers to be served their milk by the jug-ful. By the dress and the style of motor vehicle (extreme left) the time is the early 1920s. The shop behind the milk lorry is Mack's Stores, which sold clothes and toys amongst other items. In 1913, as an inducement, the proprietors reimbursed the cost of tram fares paid by cus-tomers from outlying villages. Ladies' fleece-lined coats sold for 15/11d and blouses for 3/11d. Its toy department was 'second to none in Scotland'. After closure in 1924, the premises were taken over by Budge, the drapers.

18   The Burgh Chambers, completed in 1879, are a focal point in this High Street scene. Originally, the architect intended that the tower reach only as far as the four turrets. The city fathers in their wisdom decided otherwise, having the tower raised by 117 feet in order that the clock faces be more widely seen. In the earlier postcard (left) the corner shop on the right, C. Murie & Son, sold ready-made clothing for men, youths and boys. We note that a Gospel Hall is above this store. By the time of the right-hand card (1920s), the Dunfermline Co-operative Society had moved into this site with a ground floor shop and signs up above advertising their luncheon and tea rooms. The Scot Shoe House occupied the shop on the opposite corner. Next to it, we see a second café with lunch and tea rooms and, across the street on the south side, we see yet another catering establishment.

19   In 1911 John Scott, on the left of the trio on the right-hand picture, started his family butcher's business at No. 25-27 High Street. Notice the butcher's steels (knife sharpeners) hanging from their belts. Placards proclaim his wares which included salt tongues, ham and bacon, and corned beef. Jimmy Chalmers was one of his delivery men, driving out to the suburbs and surrounding villages. This delivery cart (picture below) was No. I. The heavy clothing on the seat provided the only protection against inclement weather. The whistle hanging from Jimmy's money-bag strap was used to announce his presence. It is a smart turnout – man, horse and vehicle alike – proclaiming that John Scott sells a quality product.

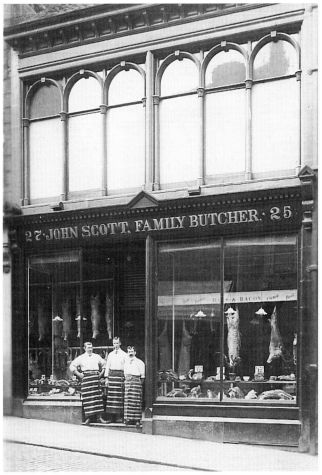

20 This advertisement card was posted in 1906. The shop was at the west end of the High Street next to Blelloch's Close. The advertisement captions were added to the original photograph. The writer of the captions obviously could not spell very well. The name Jock is curiously spelt. As well as tobacco and pipes, the owner sold a variety of newspapers and magazines, including 'The Christian Herald', 'The Boys Realm', 'Photo Bits' and 'Pathfinder'. Later views show the shop renamed 'The Wee Sweetie Shop'.

21   This procession took place in February 1899 to mark the return of the Earl of Elgin from India, where he had served for five years as Viceroy and Governor-General. A keen Liberal politician, the ninth earl served as colonial secretary from 1905 to 1908. Notice the bunting, the huge crowd and the soldiers lining the causied road. Up above, virtually every window is occupied.

22   Taken from the same location a decade or so later, this postcard view shows that various shop fronts, including Lipton's, have been modernised. The tramway, of course, is now in operation. The extension to Rumblingwell was opened in December 1913 with a High Street speed limit of 8 m.p.h. Observe how obtrusive the advertising boards are, especially those above Tyler's boot and shoe emporium. Apart from the tramcar and a hand-cart, every vehicle is horse-drawn. These include a lorry on the right and, by the tram, a gig with two passengers.

High Street, Dunfermline

23 Bridge Street, circa 1900, was a prestigious shopping street. Observe the sun canopies, some of them supported on upright poles. The shops include a cabinetmaker's, a watchmaker's, and one selling Singer's sewing machines. Eddie's (bottom picture – a mid-1920s photograph) was the retail outlet for the Dunfermline Cabinet and Upholstery Works, which were then located in Golfdrum Street. The girl in the photograph, Mary Baxter, is still with us, in her nineties and living in Dunfermline. This shop stood next to the City Hotel. On the other side, we see a fine array of flat bunnets on sale at W. & J. McLaren's, outfitters and drapers.

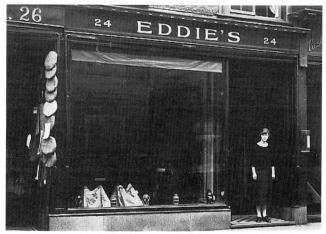

24   Still on Bridge Street, we observe how this thoroughfare was altered when the Louise Carnegie Gates were constructed in the late 1920s. The buildings nearest the camera on both sides (including the Fairfield Drapery Stores) were demolished at that time. Note that in the right-hand 1950s picture, David Hutton's drapery now occupies the corner site. On the other side, we see Bruce and Glen's grocery which is still remembered for the evocative smell of ground coffee. Neither of these firms remain in business. Next to Hutton's we observe Coull and Matthew's ironmongery.

25   The North Kirk was opened in 1840, having cost £1,673. It was erected as part of the church extension movement of the day, which resulted from the increase in population of the town and its suburbs. Compared to the time of this postcard (circa 1930), there have been a number of small changes in the building. The weather vane, decorative finials on the steeple, the two visible lums, the iron fence, gate, and low wall have all gone. Also, the lamp above the doorway has been replaced, the street causeys have been lifted and the buildings on the extreme left have been demolished.

26   Another parade, but this time of a less militaristic nature. The occasion is the gala of 1923 when Dunfermline High School teachers and pupils, preceded by a pipe band, walked down Pittencrieff Street from Chalmers Street. In those days the procession entered the Glen via the Pittencrieff Street gates – the main entrance at that time. Again we see many spectators hinging frae the windaes. The Chalmers Street building facing the viewer was later removed to make way for the Glen Bridge completed in 1932. That building incorporated Masterton's furniture shop.

27   Now going down the Kirkgate, we pass the Star Tavern and observe a hotel on the corner where, as the next postcard shows, Fraser and Carmichael later had their warehouse. The left-hand picture is a very old one and predates 1896, when the cupola-topped Blelloch's Building was erected. Opposite the junction with the Maygate, we see on the ground-floor of the Town House the City Police Office sign. This remained a police establishment until the mid-1970s. The later postcard was sent to California in 1948. The sender enthused over her visit to this 'very old city'.

THE KIRKGATE FROM HIGH ST. DUNFERMLINE.

Kirkgate and Abbey Tower, Dunfermline.

28   The interior of Fraser and Carmichael's licensed grocery in the Maygate shows the typical shop layout of the 1930s, with goods mostly piled up on shelves behind the counters. There was no self-service in those days, the counter-staff doing all the fetching and measuring. Note the old-style scales on the right, also the ham cutter and coffee grinder. A notice boasts that their blend of pure coffee was electrically ground. Willie, the short-trousered message laddie, is posing with his message bike, a rather unusual object to find within a store. The shop and wholesale warehouse closed in January 1971.

29 In this aerial 1950s picture, we observe, left-hand side, Fraser and Carmichael's warehouse which is now demolished. Likewise gone are St. Margaret's Hall, burned down in 1961, and the kirk built as Free St. Andrew's in 1847. This church, which became South St. Andrew's, became surplus to requirements and was sold in 1954. The building was destroyed by fire in 1977. The former bus station, which was on the site of Henry Reid & Son's linen works, has since been changed into a car park. The Abbot House and its garden have, of course, been transformed into a prize-winning heritage centre.

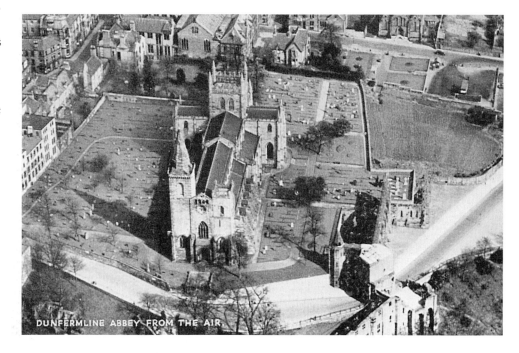

DUNFERMLINE ABBEY FROM THE AIR

30   For a change we turn to an artist's card published by the Tayport firm, the Cynicus Publishing Company. In this watercolour sketch, the artist, James Douglas RSW (1858-1911), shows us the pictur-esque rear view of the now gone tenements of St. Catherine's Wynd. Martin An-derson, 'Cynicus' himself (1854-1932), was a ken-speckle character whose barbed, satirical cartoons and postcards have always been highly appreciated by post-card collectors.

Dunfermline Abbey

31   Again we turn to an artist for an early impression of the Scottish baronial-style High School in Priory Lane, which was opened in 1886 by the Earl of Elgin. The building is now converted into flats. The postcard below, a Macpherson publication, shows us another educational establishment, the Red Tech, which was completed in 1910 as an extension to the original nearby Lauder Technical College. Again this building has been converted for other use – for housing.

Extension Lauder Technical Schools, New Row, Dunfermline

32   In the Lower Station we see a train packed with sailors, and others making their way to the platform. The sailors, in this First World War postcard, have obviously attracted a number of young ladies, one of whom is holding a child. Observe the small tearoom, an edifice which has long gone as have the gas lamp and the fences with their tin-plate adverts. Goods advertised include Sunlight Soap, Lemco, Tyler's Boots, Waverley Pens, and Robertson's Yellow Label Special Scotch Whisky.

33 Further down the New Row, we arrive at Comely Park. The scene today is rather different, since this thoroughfare is now used for parking cars. The right-hand picture, which dates from the 1950s, shows us the island building at the foot of the New Row, which was popularly known as 'The Gusset'. The Dunfermline Co-operative shop visible here was a bakery. The vehicle on the right is a police car. In recent years, the buildings were demolished when the new roundabout was constructed. With the 1870s railway viaduct now cleaned and floodlit, the southern approach to the Auld Grey Toun is now more open and attractive.

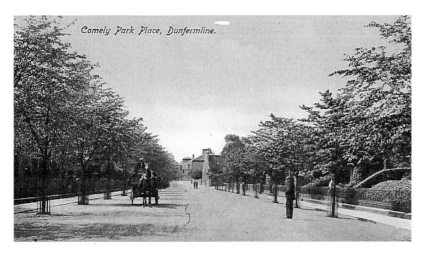

Comely Park Place, Dunfermline.

34   Moving further south, we reach an exceedingly muddy Bothwell Street. There was, of course, no filling station then – circa 1900. The part on the right, as the street sign indicates, was then named St. Leonard's Place. The tenements on the left have been demolished for street widening, work on which is still proceeding. 'The Gusset' building can be seen in the distance. As for the former St. Leonard's factory office and warehouse on the right, this has been converted into flats – Erskine Beveridge Court.

721   ST. LEONARDS FACTORY ENTRANCE, BOTHWELL STREET, DUNFERMLINE.

35   Brucefield Avenue has changed very little, except that it is now a deadend and the railings have gone. The delivery lorry belongs to a coal merchant. The card, posted in May 1915, tells an interesting story. The sender had been on a vessel which had been 'stopped on our road to America by submarines and had to make for Liverpool'. From there he sailed as a fireman (stoker) to Rosyth on the battle-cruiser H.M.S. 'Tiger' (see No. 100 in volume I). The 'Tiger', which had suffered some damage at the battle of Dogger Bank in January, had presumably sailed to Liverpool for repairs, since Rosyth dockyard was not then operational. The sender added: 'Will be in the North Sea very soon as the boat is under orders.'

Brucefield Avenue, Dunfermline.   Christie.

36   Still on the south side, we are now looking up a much altered Moodie Street. Apart from Carnegie's birthplace, every one of the Moodie Street properties has been demolished. The date, judging by the ladies' outfits, is the mid-1920s. Traffic on the causied streets was light, so there was no need for traffic lights. In fact, the only vehicle to be seen is a bicycle. Fry's Chocolate, Rowntree's Chocolate, Sunlight Soap and Watson's Matchless Soap were among the products advertised at the corner shop.

Moodie Street, Dunfermline.

37   Now we move to a close-up view of Andrew Carnegie's birthplace cottage, prior to the completion of the Memorial Hall in 1928. The horse-drawn lorry belongs to R. Douglas, lemonade manufacturer. Are the laddies minding the horse? Notice the reins dangling down to the road. The advert on the gable draws attention to a now defunct newspaper. 'The Rosyth & Forth Mail'. This is another building which has been converted into housing.

Carnegie's Birthplace, Dunfermline

38   This post-1918 card (below) takes us inside Carnegie's cottage to the up-stairs room where he was born. The portrait and the two busts above the fireplace are of Andrew Carnegie himself. Since then, the room has been redesigned in a more realistic fashion to recreate the appear-ance of an 1830s interior. Andrew Carnegie enriched Dunfermline by creating the Carnegie Dunfermline Trust. His lawyer and first chairman of the trust was John Ross, shown here in a posed photo-graph taken by James Norval. Norval, of course, was Ross's succesor as chairman and also shared the dinstinction of being knighted.

Liddell, Printer.]   **JOHN ROSS, Esq., LL.D.,**   [Norval, Photo.
Chairman, Carnegie Dunfermline Trust.

39 Alexander's bus station, mentioned in caption No. 29, now comes into closer focus. The style of the cars and buses suggests the mid-1930s. It is interesting to note that, even at that early date, part of the site was being used as a car park. Vera, who posted this card to her sister, rather belatedly admitted that she had forgotten to tell her that she had taken £1 out of their father's till on Friday. She further stated that she was having a great time – presumably spending the cash she had appropriated from the till.

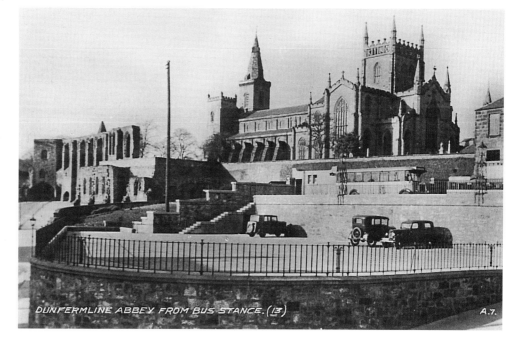

DUNFERMLINE ABBEY FROM BUS STANCE. (13)

A.7.

40   In the early 1900s, the Palace was, as now, one of Dunfermline's tourist attractions. The scene shown here is greatly altered since these photographs were taken before the excavations of 1913-1915, which revealed hitherto concealed details of the structure. The floor level in the right-hand card has since been lowered to reveal the original vaults. With regard to the card below, the picturesque-looking foliage has all gone, whilst parts of the original structure have been consolidated.

41 Turning now to the Glen, we see the original wooden bandstand and tea house. The bandstand was built in 1904 soon after Andrew Carnegie's gift of the park to the people of the Auld Grey Toun. For long, it was the policy of the Carnegie Dunfermline Trust to provide musical performances to implement Carnegie's desire to bring 'sweetness and light into the monotonous lives of the toiling masses'. The tea house in the background was likewise erected in 1904. After extension in 1907, it was removed and replaced by the present building in 1927.

DUNFERMLINE.
TEA HOUSE, PITTENCRIEFF GLEN.

42   We now see the band kiosk, which replaced the first bandstand in 1909. The kiosk, which was replaced by the Music Pavilion in 1935, was demolished and the site is now a car park. In 1905 the Carnegie Dunfermline Trust set up its own band, illustrated here, under the leadership of bandmaster Alexander Jordan. In the days before radio and television, the Military Band, as it was termed, gave performances which attracted large crowds. This band continued until 1920. As we see from the postcard, a variety of instruments were employed, including woodwind.

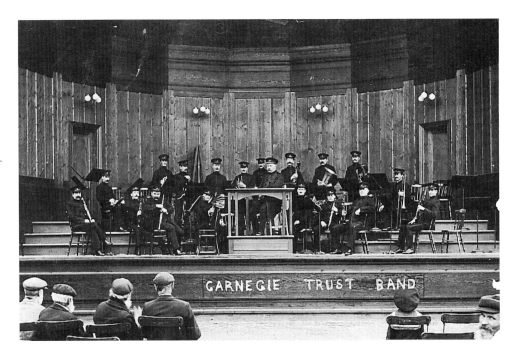

43　This gala day photograph was taken in the late 1920s prior to the construction of the Music Pavilion. Ladies' cloche hats and fox furs, men's plus-fours, and boys' caps, blazers and shorts evoke the period. Despite the presence of two parkies and waste-paper bins, there is a considerable amount of litter lying around. This tea-house was opened in 1927. Notice the builders' ladders and materials left close to the balcony.

TEA-HOUSE, PITTENCRIEFF PARK, DUNFERMLI

44   Notice the change in men's and ladies' fashions in this earlier gala day photograph by James Norval. Sailor-type suits were then in vogue for both boys and girls. Is the laddie waving an American flag to mark the American connection through Carnegie? Although James Norval, who was Provost of Dunfermline from 1918 to 1924, and Andrew Shearer, who was Town Clerk, are formally dressed, they are both sooking away at ice-cream cones as are all the other adults.

45 James Norval is featured again in the centre of the photograph showing the official opening of the Louise Carnegie Gates on the 28th of June 1929. Three local schoolgirls, all named Margaret – as were Carnegie's mother, daughter and granddaughter – cut the ribbons for the ceremonial opening. The second photo shows the aftermath at the band kiosk when the three Margarets were each presented with gold wrist watches. In this photograph, ex-Provost James Norval is making the presentation to wee Margaret Campbell aptly described as 'the tiniest morsel of all'. Notice the astute use of advertising by James Scott & Co., Electrical Engineers and Radio Manufacturers, Dunfermline and Perth.

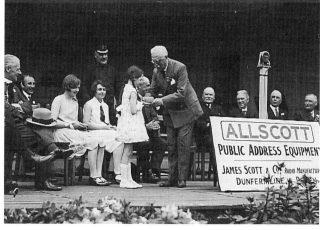

46 These are the original greenhouses which were in place when Andrew Carnegie purchased the Glen in 1902. In 1911 the Carnegie Dunfermline Trust replaced these hothouses, 'old friends' as they were described. The old greenhouses, as we can see from the postcard, were small – too narrow for easy public access, and more importantly, they were falling down due to 'the destroying hand of time'. The 1911 conservatories in their turn gave way to the buildings, which are now one of the Glen's foremost attractions.

THE GARDENS PITTENCRIEFF GLEN. DUNFERMLINE.

R.R.R.
E.

47   Another of the Glen's summer attractions is featured in this postcard which was posted to Glasgow in 1953. 'This is the place for a good rest,' the sender wrote. Contrast the adults' formal attire with the bairns' more carefree garb. This pool was constructed in 1934. The design is typical of the period. So popular was this pond that a second pool was later added.

PADDLING POOL, PITTENCRIEFF GLEN, DUNFERMLINE.   B.2529.

48 This postcard, which is of the same period as the previous card, shows Pittencrieff House, whose ground floor was adapted as a museum in 1905. Observe the 'Ambition Statue' of a bronze figure of a youth beside the mansion. Erected in 1908, this statue remained a prominent feature of the park until recent years. Due to theft and vandalism, it was removed for safe keeping and, regrettably, is no longer on display.

PITTENCRIEFF PARK, DUNFERMLINE.

49   The Town Brass Band played at many social occasions as it still does to this day. Its origins go back to 1892, when a bazaar was held to raise funds to purchase instruments and uniforms. In 1905 the band ran into problems when the town council withdrew its support. It was reformed in the following year when 18 instruments were bought. This postcard probably dates back to that time. The big drum, which still survives, was one of these new instruments. Note that not all the players wear uniforms. Moustaches, though, it must be said, were very much in favour in the early 1900s. Observe, too, that unlike today the band is all male.

Dunfermline Town Brass Band.   Photo. by Frazer & Anderson.

50 Observe in the left-hand illustration how few houses there are in the Garvock Hill area. The Public Park was, as we have previously observed, utilised as 'a lung' by the working people of Dunfermline. In the postcard on the left we see some laddies playing cricket. In the other photograph the bandstand is occupied and a large assembly has gathered to listen to the band. The costumes point to the Edwardian period. Notice, too, the number of bicycles in the foreground. In recent years the park has been bisected by the dual carriageway of Queen Margaret Drive.

338 Public Park and Park Place, Dunfermline

Band Stand, Public Park, Dunfermline.

51   Dunfermline folk did not spend all their leisure time at home. The availability of motor buses meant that holidays could be spent at a variety of destinations, including in this instance the Borders or 'Scott Country' as it was popularly termed. The occasion was the annual Wayzgoose of the employees of 'The Dunfermline Press'. A Wayzgoose is the traditional name given to a printers' outing. The snapshot below was taken at St. Mary's Loch and the bus was provided by a local firm, Simpsons & Forresters Ltd. of Market Street, Dunfermline.

MOTOR TOUR

The Dunfermline Press

MONDAY, 18th JUNE 1934

THE SCOTT COUNTRY

52 Ice hockey was a highly popular spectator sport in this area from 1939 until 1955, when Dunfermline Ice Rink closed. The rink seated 3,400 spectators, including many service personnel from Rosyth and other local naval and military bases. The local club, as we see from the programme, was called the Vikings. Matches against other Scottish teams, including local rivals the Fife Flyers from Kirkcaldy, were keenly contested. As the advertisement of the late 1940s shows, other sports and activities, including skating and curling, were catered for.

53 The photograph illustrates a Vikings team of that period. Many of the players were imported from Canada. Local stars included Johnny Rolland and the brothers Tuck and Tiny Syme, coal miners from Blairhall. Whilst Tuck Syme played for Great Britain in the 1948 Winter Olympics, Johnny Rolland represented Britain in the 1950 and 1951 World Championships. An outstanding Canadian was Nebby Thrasher. Notice the Viking head emblazoned on the team's jerseys.

54 Boxing too had its devotees. Willie Cuthbertson, shown here with a fine array of trophies, was a very popular local amateur. In 1920 he became Scottish amateur flyweight champion. In the same year he was placed third at his weight at the Olympic Games in Antwerp. The following year he won the British championship. In 1923 he turned professional, becoming a booth boxer. In 1925, after his retiral from the ring, he became a boxing instructor at the Carnegie Gym in Dunfermline and at Craigflower Private School at Torryburn.

55 Now to a show-time occasion with, on display at Broomhead Park, two fine horse-drawn vehicles – on the left a Scott, the butcher's van, and, right, Willie Best's fruit and vegetable lorry. In the lower, and older, photograph we see a lorry owned by Mutter Howie, a well-known contractor. The lorry in this 1912 Inglis Street view is carrying four huggets i.e. hogsheads or casks each containing 54 gallons of beer.

56 Many horses were actually hired both for pleasure and business from local firms, such as John Goodall, a firm which started in Commercial School Lane in 1869 with one horse and one cab. It grew in size until even the local fire brigade were hiring horses from this Queen Anne Street firm. This carefully-posed photograph was taken in 1902 on Halbeath Road. As can be seen from this late 1960s photograph (right) Goodall's made the successful transition from horse-drawn vehicles to motor vehicles. The firm and building alike have now gone, the site being incorporated in the Kingsgate Centre.

57   The left-hand postcard also has a Queen Anne Street connection. We see an obviously brand new vehicle of the Queen Anne Street firm of P. Strachan & Sons, Dunfermline and Glasgow carriers. The photograph was taken at Kirkcaldy harbour. The vehicle is a Manchester 30 cwt. lorry, bodywork by David Ronaldson of Kirkcaldy. Another 1920s vehicle is the DCI Morris van photographed in Woodmill Street below Dunfermline Lower Station. The lad is James Turpie and the woman is Christina Cross (Mrs. Johnstone). During the First World War she had the distinction of being DCI's first lady motor mechanic and driver.

58   The Dunfermline & District Tramways Company started operations in 1909 and served the public well until final closure in July 1937. The top postcard features Tram No. 21, which was delivered in 1910. In this early 1920s card, we see John Anderson, the driver, with an unknown conductress. In the excellent D.L.G. Hunter photograph, taken in 1936, we see Car No. 2 at St. Leonard's Depot (lower photograph). Note on this car the extra safety rails on the top deck and the different position of the destination board. All Dunfermline trams were altered in this way in the early 1920s. Notice the extensive overhead wire network above the tramcar.

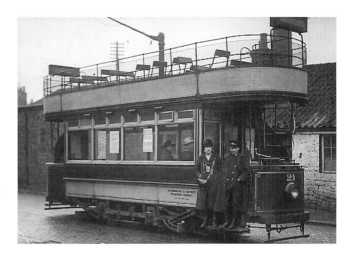

59   In this striking photograph we see a local bus conductress, Belle McConnell, in front of a Tillings-Stevens bus (known locally as Tillies). This particular vehicle, which was new in 1924, was built for the Dunfermline & District Tramways Company. It was a 40 horse-power 26-seat vehicle. Later the company's buses were managed by the Scottish General Omnibus Company. This photograph was taken in Pilmuir Street, opposite the Baths, which was the terminus for the Dunfermline to Saline route.

60   Pittencrieff Street is the place where the photograph of the Scottish General Bus Company's Leyland Lion bus has been taken. John Duffy, wearing civvies, later became a bus inspector with Alexander's. On one occasion, during 1927, John Duffy was charged with a driving offence, namely: speeding at a ferocious speed exceeding 12 miles per hour. (The speed limit for buses was raised to 20 m.p.h. in 1930.) The vehicle he was driving at the time appears in the previous picture. The other picture is slightly later – 1931. The bus is a Morris Viceroy, the bodywork built by John Jackson & Sons, coachbuilders, Pittencrieff Street. The location is the Fife Motor Company's premises in Halbeath Road. This building, as with the Pittencrieff Street dwellings shown in the other photograph, is now no more.

61   From road transport we turn to rail with two photographs of the former Upper Station taken in 1985 by co-author Eric Simpson. By then the office buildings had been boarded up and were out of use. The line from Dunfermline to Stirling was opened in 1850 connecting with the Edinburgh, Perth and Dundee Railway. Later the North British Railway Company took over these lines. Now we have, on and around this site, the Carnegie Retail Park, the Sheriff Court and Dunfermline Police Station.

62   The railway line in this illustration was completed in 1877 to provide a direct link, via a ferry at Queensferry, between Dunfermline and Edinburgh. Local industries, e.g. the Bothwell Linen Works (the two-storey building on the left), benefited from improved means of communication with raw materials coming in and finished goods going out. On the west side of Elgin Street can be seen some of the buildings of the Elgin Bleachfield.

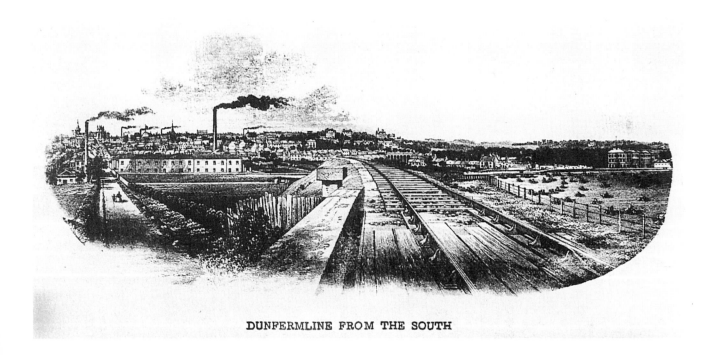

DUNFERMLINE FROM THE SOUTH

63   We now see, in more detail, the Bothwell Linen Works which, founded in 1865, was one of Dunfermline's early power-loom factories. Prominent in this picture is the mill's big lum. The pond in the foreground belonged to the Elgin Bleachfield. It was fed with water drawn from the Lyne Burn, which can just be seen on the north side of the pond. The burn is now partially culverted. A copious, clean water supply was essential for the boiling and bleaching processes employed at the Elgin Works.

64 Returning to the north side of the town to what was then North (later Upper) Station Road, we come to Wilson's embroidery works. This once prominent firm, started by James and Robert Wilson in 1919, closed in 1963. The founders' father, also James Wilson, was a partner in the local textile firm of Wilson & Wightman. Mr. Wilson senior, a man with an inventive turn of mind, perfected the embroidery machine and a spraying device. The ornate letter-heading is typical of the period.

Telephone No. 451. Telegrams: "Needlework, Dunfermline". Code used: A.B.C. 5th Edition.

Sole Partner:- ROBERT WILSON.

Wilson Brothers

EMBROIDERY
MANUFACTURERS
OF FANCY LINENS
AND ART SILK
FABRICS

North Station Road,
DUNFERMLINE 14th October 19 39

65   Meal mills and flour mills were important for the local economy, but in the 19th century with the building of new, large factory-type mills many small water mills became uneconomic. Thus Dunfermline's famous Heugh Mills which were perched one above another in the Glen lost their trade and were abandoned. The photo shows the topmost mill as it was in the early 1900s. The mill lay below the First World War memorial in Monastery Street.

66 Elder's lorry has been loaned for charitable purposes to raise money for lifeboats. Hugh Elder's firm has seized the opportunity to advertise their products, the sacks on view being labelled respectively barley, wheat and oats. Observe the sheafs and flags adorning the lorry. The building in the background is, we presume, their granary in Queen Anne Street which preceded their Inglis Street mill. The business was founded in 1834 by David Elder, who was succeeded by Hugh Elder. This particular firm of Hugh Elder & Son Ltd. went into voluntary liquidation in 1968.

Macintyre, Photo. *Duntermlin*

LIFEBOAT DEMONSTRATION, 1903.
HUGH ELDER, GRAIN AND SEED MERCHANT, DUNFERMLINE.

67   Brown's Laundry staff are here photographed in the 1930s. The premises were situated in Grieve Street and the buildings are now occupied by a timber merchant's, Magnet Ltd. The employees are mostly very tidy and well-groomed. Notice too the van drivers' smart uniforms and caps. The two laddies who are wearing caps are van boys. The youngish man seated in the front row (sixth from the left) is the boss – Willie Brown.

68   We now turn to another staff photograph taken in the linotype room of the Dunfermline Press which was then based in the New Row. The photograph displays machinery and techniques of printing that are now very much of the past. It was taken on a Monday morning when the workshop staff had just cleared the previous week's newspaper and were now preparing to start on the next issue. The galleys (long trays) to the right contain unused letters. On the left are three of the four linotype machines which were used in the hot metal process. The editor, William Kirk, stands slightly apart on the right. In the front row, third from the left, sits David Harrison, who finally retired from the Press in 1981.

69   In the 19th century mining provided a great deal of work for the folk of Dunfermline and surrounding area. One of the major pits was the Wellwood Colliery, which continued in operation until 1950. The pithead had been destroyed by fire so the workings were closed. The photograph is a very rare early one, showing Wellwood colliers posing at the end of a shift for Dunfermline photographer A. Dewar. Since mining was very thirsty work, the miners are carrying their metal flasks, which usually were filled with cold tea. Notice that there are no safety helmets and only primitive lamps fixed to their bunnets.

70   There were so many miners in this part of Fife that the headquarters of the Fife Miners' Association was established in Dunfermline. Stained glass windows adorned the union's Victoria Street premises. The picture inscribed 'Modern Workings' shows one of these windows now held by Dunfermline's Viewfield Museum. One of the leading figures in the miners' union, Halbeath-born Willie Adamson (1863-1936), is shown here in 1924 being presented with the freedom of the 'City and Royal Burgh of Dunfermline' by Provost James Norval. William Adamson, a Baptist and teetotaller, had become Labour M.P. for West Fife in 1910 and was made Secretary for Scotland in the first Labour administration in 1924. He later became Secretary of State for Scotland and served in this office until 1931.

71   This photograph was taken a few years earlier, in 1919, at the time of another freedom ceremony. The recipient, third from the left in the rear row, is Admiral David Beatty (1871-1936), who had commanded the British Grand Fleet in the later stages of the First World War. The Dunfermline connection was obviously due to the major part of the fleet being based at Rosyth. When on shore, Admiral Beatty resided in the village of Aberdour in Aberdour House (see 'Aberdour and Burntisland in old picture postcards' caption 35). The party includes the Town Clerk Andrew Shearer (extreme left), Provost Norval (next to Beatty), and the Earl of Elgin (extreme right).

72   The year is 1923 and we go now to the Lower Railway Station for the arrival of a royal party to Dunfermline for the purpose of visiting the Abbey and Carnegie Trust buildings. It was the first royal visit to the Auld Grey Toun since Charles II in 1650. The king, George V, is obscured by the Duchess of York (now the Queen Mother) who, as ever, is aware of the presence of a press photographer. Queen Mary stands on her left and on her right is the Duke of York, later George VI.

73   The king, accompanied by the Earl of Elgin, leads the party on a 'walkabout', while going along Bath Street (now part of Pilmuir Street) from the Carnegie Baths to the Women's Institute. Observe that, on this sunny July day, the royals are wearing white gloves, the purpose being to protect their hands. Although one soldier is visible, there is no obvious police presence. In all, an estimated 30,000 spectators lined the streets of Dunfermline. In honour of the occasion, a triumphal arch was erected in the Kirk-gate.

74   The party later proceeded to Pittencrieff Park to plant trees to commemorate their majesties' visit to the ancient royal burgh. Notice the cameraman in the background. Local schoolgirls, chosen by ballot, presented bouquets to the royal ladies. The flowers being presented to the duchess are pink roses from the park gardens. Again the Duchess Elizabeth is well aware of the presence of a photographer.

75   We go now to what is now the Leyspark Private Nursing Home. During the First World War this building was used as a temporary military hospital, where local volunteers, with professional help, looked after sick and wounded military personnel. V.A.D. stands for Voluntary Aid Detachment. Prior to the Great War, this was the Poor House for the Dunfermline area. Hospital wards were an integral feature of poorhouses of this size and type. Later, it was transformed into the Northern Hospital. No doubt some of the military veterans seen standing in the background in the previous photograph passed through this, or similar, V.A.D. hospitals.

Wartime food shortages meant that empty spaces and ornamental gardens, as we see here, were utilised to grow vegetables.

V.A.D. HOSPITAL, DUNFERMLINE.

76   Looking down Townhill Road (this part then named Downieville Crescent) we see a greatly-altered scene. Some of the buildings on the left have gone and the dwellings on the right have given way to the Police Station and Halfords. Prominent in the distance is Bennachie, the large house with the spire, which was the home of Sir William Robertson of the large linen manufacturing company Hay and Robertson. Nowadays, it is used for Fife Council purposes. In 1909, trams commenced on this route, running to Townhill from East Port. When the kirks were in on Sundays, all cars went no further than the Park Gates.

DOWNIEVILLE CRESCENT, DUNFERMLINE.

77   Halfway up Townhill Road looking north, we see the single track tramline heading for Townhill. Because of the steep hills, only experienced drivers were employed on this route. The benefits conveyed by the introduction of trams were considerable, speeds of up to 16 m.p.h. being possible on open stretches. It should be noted that the maximum allowable speed for motor buses at this time was 12 m.p.h. (See No. 60.) The tramway service opened up job opportunities for people living in outlying villages and towns. Workers' specials started as early as 4.40 a.m.

TOWNHILL RD. FROM ROSS ST. DUNFERMLINE.

78   At the top of Townhill Road we see a high wall shielding the house where lived the redoubtable Reverend Jacob Primmer (1842-1914). This bible-thumping preacher was the Church of Scotland minister at Townhill, who was notorious for his anti-Catholic opinions and demonstrations. The manse was built by the Church of Scotland in 1903 and it was occupied by 'Jaikie' Primmer from then until his death in 1914. Note that two tram cars are heading up Townhill Road.

TOWNHILL ROAD LOOKING TOWARDS DUNFERMLINE.

79   As the Townhill postcard and the 1910 letter heading indicate, the Lochside Coal & Fireclay Company covered an extensive area. Although Townhill was well known for its coal pits, the rich beds of local fireclay proved to be an exceedingly valuable commodity. Fireclay goods included chimney cans and various types of pipes. Observe, to the right in the letter heading, two kilns with railway waggons close by – conveniently located for the easy transfer of bricks and other materials. The chimneys came down in 1977, work having ceased some years earlier.

Lochside Coal & Fire Clay Co. Ltd.
Telegrams:- "LOCHSIDE, TOWNHILL"   Telephone Nº119.
MANUFACTURERS of
COMPOSITION BRICKS & EVERY DESCRIPTION OF FIRE CLAY GOODS
LOCHSIDE WORKS
TOWNHILL
DUNFERMLINE   25th January 19

TOWNHILL FROM KINGSEATHILL.

80 Two generations of Townhill folk are illustrated here. In the left-hand photograph (circa 1926), we see bairns in the local primary school together with heidmaister George (Paddy) Henderson, who reigned from 1904 until 1929. The class teacher is Miss Archibald. The children are in their everyday wear. Observe how the pictures are hung – by means of long cords. In the right-hand mid-thirties photograph, we have members of Townhill Quoiting Club with an array of trophies. Playing with quoits was a very popular pastime, especially in mining communities (see also No. 60 in 'Cowdenbeath in old picture postcards'). The clubhouse, in Muir Road, was built by the members. Davie Pollock was one of the star players. Matches against local rivals, Lassodie, were keenly contested, but their champ had, we are told, 'nae chance' against Townhill's Davie.

81   Townhill Industrial Co-op was an independent institution formed because of local dissatisfaction with the Dunfermline Co-operative Society. That body had failed to support the miners when they participated in the Great Strike of 1894. The Townhill Co-op thrived to such an extent that the original single-storey building was raised to the two-storey level we see here. The date is circa 1920. The Co-op's own Shieldhall products sold here included jellies and marmalade, essence of coffee and chicory, 'Co-operative Semolina', and 'Unitas Metal Polish'.

82   In the 1920s local authorities were for the first time in their history building municipal houses to replace substandard housing stock like the miners' raws. Forest Place (here looking south) was one such scheme. However, in 1925 Townhill Pit was closed, increasing the already considerable degree of hardship in the area. The 1926 strike worsened an already parlous situation. Compared with today, the absence of private cars is a striking feature.

FOREST PLACE, TOWNHILL.

83   Preachers and police provided different types of restraint in the community. The advertising card for an evangelical preacher predates 1929, when the United Free Church was reunited with the Church of Scotland. The date of the photo (a Norval picture) showing the policemen and women is around 1943, since three of the men bear the initials W.R. (War Reserve) on their collars. The women officers belonged to another war emergency body – the Womens' Auxiliary Police Corps. The regulars from Dunfermline City Police are George Smith (back-row middle), Sandy Ruxton (front-row right) and Sergeant James Mitchell. The police office was located at the junction of Main Street and Muir Road. There is no police station in Townhill nowadays.

84   Townhill Main Street shows, on the left, the miners' raw type of building that was once so common in Fife. In this 1920s postcard, observe the carrier's lorry on the right belonging to a firm that served Kirkcaldy and Glasgow. The tramcar is coming from the Townhill terminus, which was situated halfway up Main Street.

MAIN ST., TOWNHILL.

85   In this circa 1930 postcard, the lorry on the left is parked by the tram terminus. We see, on the extreme right, the Post Office and stationery and newsagent's business of Robert Wilson. This Townhill shopkeeper served on Dunfermline Town Council for 42 years, being Provost from 1927 till 1930. Observe the ornate Provost's lamp-posts outside his shop and abode. Townhill produced two other Dunfermline provosts, namely George Izatt (1945-1948) and Jean Mackie (1961-1964).

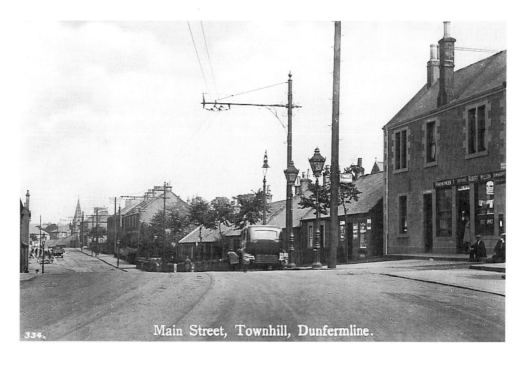

Main Street, Townhill, Dunfermline.

86 The Town Loch (Moncur) served both the industrial and recreational needs of the community. Moncur, or Moncor, was the old name for the village. Once water from the loch helped to power the flax mills of Dunfermline and gave water to the nearby brickworks. This postcard reveals how locals went there to feed the swans, also to fish and play. Nowadays with the Scottish Waterski Centre based there, the emphasis is more on recreational use.

MONCUR LOCH, TOWNHILL.

87   The date of this photo is late 1940s and most of the people in the group are miners or ex-miners. The bus driver (top right) is Geordie Robertson, father of co-author George Robertson, and the photo was taken outside the Institute. The Carnegie Institute in Townhill was erected in 1906 and was the first of its kind outwith the central area of Dunfermline. It set the pattern for the future, with a library, reading-rooms, billiard room, games room, baths and a room 'specially set aside for Ladies'! At the official opening, Trust chairman Dr. John Ross spoke of the importance of being 'well-read, especially with the recent birth of the Labour Party in Parliament'. (In that year 29 Labour Members of Parliament were elected to the House of Commons.)

88 Going now to the west side of Dunfermline, we arrive at what is nowadays the busy dormitory village of Crossford. In this circa 1900 card we see a very different scene. Crossford was a sleepy and tranquil small village, with flocks of sheep providing the sole traffic hazard. The houses lay mainly alongside the main road. Since this time, new private housing estates have changed the appearance of this onetime weaving village.

89   It was the coming of the motor car that transformed the village of Crossford, allowing commuters easy access to Dunfermline and other large centres. Wilson's garage shown here, the second in the village, was built in 1932. While the site, by the traffic lights, is still in use, the original garage building was demolished in 1984 and the site was later redeveloped. The car is thought to be of American manufacture and the owner, we are told, is the man on the left – Geordie McDonald. The garage proprietor, Willie Wilson, stands in the middle. The petrol and oil products are all Esso.

90 Looking eastward along Main Street towards Dunfermline, we see in the left-hand picture a Crossford which, although the road has been upgraded, has changed very little. With only one bus in sight, the village is still relatively free of traffic. In the previous century, some of the small dwellings, one with window shutters, would have accommodated weavers' looms. In the right-hand postcard, we are looking southward towards the back of Main Street with, beyond, Waggon Road. This picture predates the garage in No. 89 and emphasises the rural nature of the village.

91 At the beginning of the 20th century, Carnock was another tiny and quiet rural centre with crow-stepped gables and pantile roofs. Apart from the building on the extreme right, the immediate scene has changed but little. The buildings on the left, incorporating the Old Inn, have been modernised, as have the cottages on Carneil Road in the centre of the picture. Beyond the Old Inn, the exterior of the present Post Office shows comparatively little change, even to the guttering running across the gable window.

Main Street, Carnock.

92   Proceeding further west out on the Alloa Road, we arrive at Comrie. It looks as if the entire population of the hamlet has turned out to meet the photographer. The women are dressed for work: they are all wearing long pinnies. Since the time of this card (postmark date 1907), Comrie has been greatly expanded. The tall post on the right side is a puzzle. Can anyone tell us what its function was?

COMRIE VILLAGE, OAKLEY. W.G.M.

93   As we see from this early 1900s photograph of what, we understand, is Oakley sawmill, this industry employed quite a few men. Oakley had developed because of the rapid expansion of the Forth or Oakley Ironworks (1845-1869). Obviously, by the time this photo was taken the iron works had closed. The sawmill, then owned by J. & T. Young, occupied part of the site of the ironworks to the west of Station Road. As well as cut timber for surface construction, the local pits used a lot of timber for underground galleries. The men's breeks, it may be noted, are supported by galluses.

94   Proceeding eastward to the Firth of Forth, we view West Fife from the south. In this post-First World War postcard, the large warship (an American ship?) is heading up the firth towards Rosyth. Between Inverkeithing and North Queensferry, the Port Laing or Government Pier was still intact and remained in use for some time thereafter. Although. St David's appears, there is no town of Dalgety Bay. We see, however, the hangars of Donibristle airfield.

95   Donibristle, or Donibee, was a major employer in the area. Starting off as a First World War airfield on the Earl of Moray's Donibristle Estate, its workshops were developed during the Second World War for the repair of naval aircraft. From 1939 to 1945, Donibee housed a shore base for naval aircraft and a largely civilian-staffed Royal Naval Aircraft repair yard. Donibristle's role as an operational air station, H.M.S. 'Merlin', came to an end in 1953. The repair yard, one section of which is illustrated here, continued till 1959. In place of the yard and airfield site, we now have industrial estates and the streets and dwellings of the new town of Dalgety Bay.

96   Donibristle air base started as an offshoot of Rosyth naval base and dockyard. It was deep water and a sheltered location that attracted naval planners to the Rosyth area. As we see from the top picture, which predates construction work on the dockyard, quarrying was a local industry with limestone shipped out from the jetty seen here. It was in this area that oil storage tanks were constructed. In the background, we can just see Rosyth Castle, which features more prominently in the artist's illustration (postmark date 1904) below. Notice the picturesque nature of the scene which was a popular spot with local holiday-makers.

St. Margaret's Hope, Naval Base.

ROSYTH CASTLE, ST. MARGARET'S HOPE.
The site of the new Naval Base in the Forth.

97   It is now a very different time. This card was posted in September 1914 when the Great War had just started. Flagwaving is now the order of the day. Note the nautical emphasis of this typical patriotic card, which has Rosyth Castle as its centrepiece. The young laddie who despatched this card to an Edinburgh pal had been having 'a ripping time with plenty of fishing'. As an afterthought, he enquires: 'What do you think of the war?'

98 'Rosyth's All Right' exclaims this dapper naval personage as he surveys the quayside scene. The reason for this congratulatory cartoon is explained by the adjacent drawing. These artist's impressions decorate a menu card for a celebratory dinner held by the builders' Messrs. Easton Gibb & Son Ltd. The builders had started work in 1909 and by April 1916 they had completed an important stage in the construction process. This was the completion of an emergency entrance and the main ship channel allowing major vessels to enter the basin.

99   Since this card was made out to Mr. James Beveridge who occupied seat number 452, this was obviously a well-attended function. Despite wartime shortages, the menu, listed on the reverse side, was surprisingly extensive with no fewer than seven courses followed by coffee. In the chair was the boss of this Monmouth-based firm: Alexander Gibb. Not surprisingly, the toast-list commenced with 'The King' followed by the 'Imperial Forces'. The last toast was to 'The Ladies' and significantly they were not allowed to speak for themselves. Their reply was given by one of the male guests, a Mr. Last!

100   When complete, the dockyard and its workshops covered an extensive area. Rail communications were of vital importance. Note the tank engine to the right and the NB (North British Railway Company) wagons. Observe too the massive piles of iron anchor chains in the foreground.

VIEW OF WORKSHOPS, ROSYTH DOCKYARD.

Copyright
R.D.4.

101   Rosyth in the later stages of the war housed the British Grand Fleet, whose major warships were battleships and battlecruisers. H.M.S. 'Courageous', which is shown here in No. 2 Dock, was a very fast, light battlecruiser with four 15 inch guns as her main armament. She suffered some damage and casualties in action with enemy light forces in November 1917. As a battlecruiser her tripod mast and single funnel were readily identifiable features. In 1924-1928 she was converted into an aircraft carrier. Sunk by a German U-boat on 27 September 1939, she was the first Royal Navy vessel to be destroyed in that war. Of her crew, 514 were lost.

H.M.S. "Courageous" in No 2 Dock, Rosyth

102 The Cunard White Star Liner, the 'Mauretania', held the Blue Riband for the fastest crossing of the Atlantic for many years. But in this photograph, she has reached her last destination, arriving at No. 1 drydock, Rosyth, in July 1935. By this time the naval base was operating on a care and maintenance basis and part of the yard had been let to Metal Industries Ltd. for shipbreaking. Sightseers were permitted on board, with boarding charges going to charity. On one Sunday well over 10,000 visitors visited the vessel. Alarm, however, was expressed by the amount of damage caused by souvenir hunters. Interestingly enough, a later 'Mauretania' was broken up at Ward's in Inverkeithing.

THE MAURETANIA AT ROSYTH

103   Accommodation for construction workers was obviously an essential requirement. 'Rosyth Village', or Tintown, as it was more popularly known, housed many of the new Rosyth workforce. During one month in 1913, 54 temporary dwellings were erected by the contractors, Easton Gibb. That particular batch of huts came from a newly-completed railway project at Immingham Docks. The back of the card gives a short description of the new village, which, we are told, enjoyed a 'dry, healthy and bracing' climate. 'Food is cheap,' we are also told, 'and rents are low.' No wonder rents were low, for these corrugated iron huts had no gas or electricity, no baths, no hot water and no indoor toilets – just a dry closet in the garden.

Portion of Rosyth Village

104 Still at Tintown, we see one of John Scott's butcher vans outside one of the buildings. Visiting vans were welcomed, there being few shops in the village. (For further information about this High Street firm, see No. 19.) Doubtless aware that the workforce was of an itinerant nature, goods were sold at the van on a cash basis only. Observe the driver's muddy boots and the butcher's steel (for sharpening knives) in his hand.

105   As well as the temporary houses of Tintown, permanent dwellings were also erected, since the dockyard plans were to incorporate a new town built on Garden City principles. We see here some of these houses in course of erection on Castlandhill. We are looking north towards Admiralty Road and the Crossroads. Prior to the construction of Admiralty Road, this had been the main road between North Queensferry and Dunfermline.

Rosyth from Castlandhill.

106   The house on the extreme right in the previous photo is featured again in this 1930s postcard. Notice, in this card, the idiosyncratic spelling of Castlandhill. In the early 1930s few residents possessed motor vehicles. Compare this street scene with that of today. Nowadays, the streets are filled with vehicles, both moving and stationary.

Castiland Hill Road, Rosyth.

107   For residents of the new Rosyth Garden City, kirks and schools had also to be built. At the foot of Castlandhill, beside the Crossroads, stands the Roman Catholic Church of St. John and St. Columba (1926). St. John's Roman Catholic School was opened in 1923. With this school building now demolished, the space is occupied by a small housing complex and Rosyth Police Call Point.

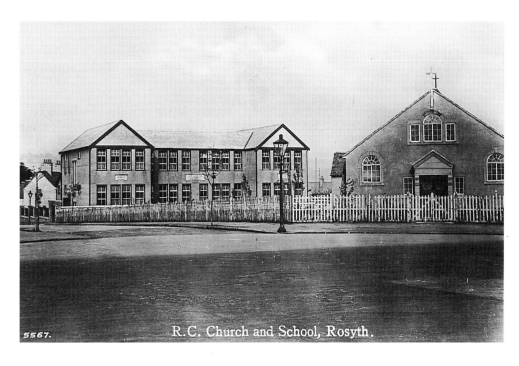

5567.

R.C. Church and School, Rosyth.

108   Beside St. John's Church, off Admiralty Road, we come to what is now Newton Place – D11 to give it its original designation. The lane leading to it was D9. In 1916, when the first permanent scheme was started, all streets were referred to by a letter and a number. Sir John Newton was one of the former landowners in the area.

Rosyth Road, D11.

109 Here we are looking north along Queesferry Road from the area of the Cross-roads. The time is the 1920s and we note once again the absence of vehicles. Since space was left for tramcar lines (never actually built), this street is extra-wide.

Queensferry Road from South.

110 Road Al became Backmarch Road, the name being derived from the nearby Backmarch Farm. Since this was to be a Garden City, front and rear gardens were intrinsic features from the start. Unlike other working class areas, all the streets we see in this and other postcards are tree-lined. The children are lined up to make sure they appear in the photograph.

111　Another of the Davidson's Silver Tone series of cards brings us to road B3, now King's Place. In the distance, we see King's Road Primary School which was opened in 1918. (See No. 112 in volume I.) What is the laddie holding? A scooter most likely!

Rosyth Road, B3.

112　In this postcard of King's and Backmarch Crescents, we see an estate where the gardens, compared to the previous photograph, have matured. As is not uncommon with postcard captions, there is a spelling mistake with one of the street names. These thoroughfares, originally numbered – B2 and A2 respectively – were two of the early streets of Rosyth Garden City. The car points to a mid-1930s date at the earliest.

Kings and Blackmarch Crescents, Rosyth.

113 The charabanc on Queensferry Road and milk cart with churns would suggest a 1920s date this time. The picture-house on the left, the Palace, dates back to 1921. In 1929 it was the first to show 'Talkies' in the Dunfermline area. Notice, at the end of Aberlour Street, the now demolished episcopal church of St. Andrew and St. George. This kirk was not completed to its original plan due to Rosyth Dockyard being reduced in 1926 to a care and maintenance basis. The original projected population of Rosyth Garden City was to have been in the region of 30,000. The kirk site is occupied by the dwellings of Mellor Court, which is a private housing association scheme. The name Wilderness Brae in the postcard caption is derived from the adjacent Wilderness Wood.

ROSYTH FROM WILDERNESS BRAE.

93082. J.V.

114   Once again a motor bus, probably an Alexander's, helps to date a photograph. The period is the late 1930s. Compared to the previous postcard, there are now a telephone kiosk and postbox (right) and there is also a shrubbery in front of the Palace Buildings. Observe the area in the foreground has now been laid out in formal fashion. The bell tower of Rosyth Parish Church, which was opened in 1931, is just visible on the left.

Queensferry Road and Palace Buildings, Rosyth.

115 Taken on the same day, the photographer has obviously swiveled his camera to the right to take in the Rosyth Hotel. Again, the area in front has been landscaped and a public toilet block erected. Rosyth Hotel (1921) was run on Gothenberg principles, thus its popular name 'The Goth'. The Rosyth Gothenberg Hotel Association, like similar tavern societies, tried to curtail excessive drinking on the part of patrons and contributed part of their profits to local community projects.

Rosyth Hotel and Aberlour Street.

116 Here we feature Queensferry Road at the junction of Parkgate – date late 1930s. A sign on the lamp-post points to Rosyth Post Office. The corner building, which is dated 1926, is occupied by Fraser & Co., family grocer, with the DCI (Dick's Co-operative Institution) opposite. Notice the delivery tricycle on the left.

A CORNER OF QUEENSFERRY ROAD, ROSYTH

117   We turn now to the paddling pool in Rosyth Public Park. This early 1950s postcard reveals how popular the pool could be, even when the weather was not terribly warm (notice the childrens' coats, cardigans and jackets). The van is a Royal Mail Morris Commercial delivery vehicle. The houses in the background are on Middlebank Street and the big lum was part of the old brickworks.

PADDLING POOL, ROSYTH.   B.4910.

118   Still on the subject of recreation, we now go to the Red Triangle Boys' Club which was located at the top of Backmarch Road. Notice the triangle symbol on the gable wall and King's Road School in the background. These premises were opened in 1918 by the Y.M.C.A. (Young Men's Christian Association), with the club continuing to operate until 1940. The Salvation Army later took over the hut. The site is now occupied by dwelling houses.

119   These young men have evidently clubbed together for a cycle run. Compared to touring models, these are bikes, including one ladies' model, which are designed for everyday practical use. The cyclists, it may be noted, are wearing their everyday clothes – no special gear for these lads, just cycle-clips. Again, the location is the top of Backmarch Road in front of Dunfermline Co-op shops, right next to the Y.M.C.A. building.

120 There is an unusually large number of police to be seen in this photograph. One must remember the date, 1944, when Rosyth dockyard was working at full pitch and the base was crammed with service personnel. Judging by their cap badges, only six belonged to the Dunfermline City Police, the rest most likely being War Reservists. The police station was at Rosyth Crossroads and is now an ex-servicemen's club.

ROSYTH POLICE, 1944.

121 The Second World War saw a great extension of the Civil Defence. The need for such an organisation continued as a result of the Cold War. Here we see some Civil Defence volunteers in a training exercise at the Palace Buildings on Queensferry Road. The date is circa mid-1950s or early 1960s. For the record, the shop on the left is Burt's, a draper's, as was the Wee Shop. Next door to it, we see what was then the North Rosyth Sub-Post Office.

122   Back to Dunfermline, we are now at the Cottage Inn at the top of the dual carriageway. Tramcar No. 36 was delivered in April 1918 by a Preston firm for use on the Rosyth route. Although vehicle construction for civilian purposes was severely constricted during the First World War, the needs of Rosyth dockyard and its workforce were evidently regarded as a war priority. As built in 1918, this was a twintrack line, running up the centre of what was the first dual carriageway in Scotland. In this 1936 D.L.G. Hunter photograph, it was not exactly the rush hour, there being only one passenger visible.

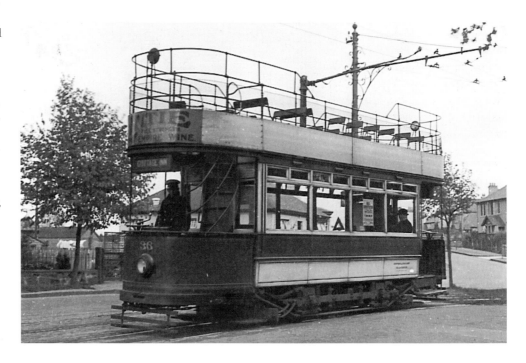

123   This type of pun on the word Greetings was very popular in the early days of postcard development. The sender is obviously addicted to this figure of speech since he makes his own awful pun in his message. This reads: 'I will leave here at 3.40 and arrive in the KIRK A'DAY (Kirkcaldy) at 4.46 so if ye can ye will but if ye canna ye winna – Much Beer.' Interestingly, the sender was confident that his card posted in Dunfermline on 24th December 1906, would be delivered in Kirkcaldy by the following day – Christmas Day!

GREETIN'S – FRAE – DUNFERMLINE

TEA ROOMS, PITTENCRIEFF GLEN.

124   Having started at the top of the New Row for our first illustration, we now return to it for our last. We are now in the mid-1960s. The number of vehicles has greatly increased and, consequently, there is now need for police control of traffic. The smartly turned-out pointsman is co-author George Robertson – at an early stage in his career with Fife Constabulary. Significantly, all the vehicles shown here are of British manufacture.